My Friend Michale
A true story about
The REAL JAWS

by
Kenneth W. Grimshaw

Copyright © 2010 Kenneth Grimshaw

All Rights Reserved.

ISBN: 0615437303

ISBN-13: 9780615437309

TO SUSAN

PART 1

Buffy, my daughter, had been fairly calm, but she was now borderline hysterical. It was 8:10 p.m., and my soul mate, Landry, had not returned. I had attempted all afternoon to stay on a northeast heading to help shorten Landry's distance to me.

How could I have been this foolish? Had my ego gotten in front of my common sense? I had been taught to be more resourceful! My hunger was not strong enough to overcome my reasoning, so why had I left myself vulnerable like that to humans? Was I just not thinking clearly?

My name is Ward; I am a great white shark. Sixteen years ago I was born just off the south shore of Long Island, New York. I lived most of the time there with my family, who for the past ten hours had been put through this unbearable heartbreak because I did not follow life's lessons.

My Friend Michale *A true story about* THE REAL JAWS

June 23, 1978, was another beautiful early summer morning in the sleepy Montauk fishing village at the eastern end of Long Island, New York. The weather was forecast to be perfect, in the mid-seventies with a light southwest wind with no fog. The charter boat *Floodtide*, an older, forty-two- foot Egg Harbor, was about to become one of the most famous fishing boats in history.

Captain Dave Sowermen and his mate, Chris Reed, readied the craft for its trip eighteen miles due south of Montauk Point to the Butterfish Hole. This is the closest point off Long Island's south shore where the depth of the ocean reaches thirty fathoms or 180 feet. On average, you have to go south one mile for each fathom; hence thirty miles south for thirty fathoms of depth.

For some reason swordfish like to come to the surface and just lie around in this depth of water. This pocket of thirty-fathom water is also called the "butterfish hole" because Montauk draggers catch large amounts of butterfish here every year. Once the local fishing season starts, the surface water tends to get warmer in this area, and many types of fish show up because of the large schools of various types of baitfish that pass through these waters. The baitfish consist of squid, herring, mackerel, bunker, and krill, sometimes in large numbers. The fish that feed on them are bonito, tuna, giant tuna, swordfish, white marlin, blue marlin, humpback whales, finback whales, pilot whales, porpoise, dolphin, and huge schools of blue fish. With this type of gourmet dining available, this area is also home to most types of North Atlantic sharks.

The *Floodtide* planned to spend the day chumming for sharks at the north end of the butterfish hole for two reasons. One, it was close to Montauk, and they did not have to run far to get there; and two, at this time of the year, blue sharks were easy to catch in these waters.

However, this day would turn out to be anything but just another day catching sharks. By tomorrow half the world population would not only have heard of Montauk from various news outlets, they would know exactly where it was! Within twenty-four hours, thousands of news media from all over the globe would invade this small town.

Most Montauk charter boats (Boats that hired out for the day or in some cases half a day) have a charter party that pays for the full day to go offshore, big-game fishing and/or shark fishing. They bring along a harpoon as part of the boat's normal equipment in case they get lucky and find a swordfish that won't take a bait. If the fish stays on the surface after they try to get it to strike a trolled squid, they then try to harpoon the swordfish. Should they get really lucky and actually land the fish aboard the boat, they can then sell it back at the dock in Montauk.

It was about seven fifteen in the morning when Sowermen's charter party showed up at the dock to board the *Floodtide*. Three of the four men in the group were already enjoying adult beverages as they got aboard. This was quite normal. For whatever reason, whenever a group of people gets together aboard a boat, some type of signal goes off and the unwritten rule is you must grab an adult beverage. They had brought enough food and drink to feed a small army; no one would go hungry aboard ship today.

Just west of the butterfish hole, in thirty fathoms of water, Chase and his much larger twin sister Susan, were digesting a small school of football-sized (less than one hundred pounds) tuna that they had come upon about ten minutes earlier.

Chase and Susan are cousins of mine. Our mothers are sisters. Kayla, my mother, is the oldest sister and I think the brightest and by far the most elegant and graceful of our immediate family. Lindsy, who is two years younger than Kayla, is Chase and Susan's mom. Our fathers have both passed away; my uncle, Brayden, was harpooned and then killed right here off Montauk some nine years ago by a boat called *The Cricket II.*

My dad, George, went missing in the Gulf of Alaska near the Hubbard Glacier just two years ago. He was very close to the face of the glacier chasing after a sea lion when the glacier suddenly carved off a humongous chunk of ice right on top of him. He knew better than to go in that close, but he was always determined to be the best and the most successful hunter in our family. I, for my own selfish reasons that year, did not make the trip all the way down the east coast of South America then back up the west coast of South America, Latin America, North America, and into the Gulf of Alaska

Kenneth W. Grimshaw

Hubbard Glacier where WARDS dad died

over twenty thousand miles altogether. This gulf is home in the North American summer to some of the best feeding grounds in the world for great white sharks.

Kenneth W. Grimshaw

You might think it is awfully cold in the Gulf of Alaska, but surface temperature of the ocean water is not something we pay much attention to because we travel down at the thermal cline where the water temperature stays the same all year around, regardless of the surface temperature. We spend most of our time at this depth. We have the ability to circulate our blood out near our skin, thereby heating or cooling our bodies almost instantly. With this gift, we can literally hunt and swim almost anywhere in any ocean, and in great white shark society, it is quite normal to roam many thousands of miles in any given season, either with a large pod of whales, giant tuna, or some other large food source. Within two years, we are always back in the area where we were born.

However, a large food supply is the only thing that really matters to us, and to be very honest with you, I'm somewhat lazy when it comes to traveling; I really did not want to make such a long, time-consuming journey that year. There was always an abundance of food and excitement right here in our own backyard.

Also at the time I had fallen in love with the loveliest young shark, caring, intelligent, and resourceful beyond any of my hopes and dreams. Without question she knew just how to flop my flippers, and she became my soul mate. Her name is Landry. We were blessed just a year ago with our first daughter, Buffy, who is truly the light of our lives.

My mom, Kayla, still mourns the loss of my father much more than I. I have several times seen a look of loneliness in her beautiful eyes that only missing Dad could account for. She was only one hundred yards from him and witnessed this heart-wrenching, horrible tragedy.

I have been blessed with a lot of my dad's instincts and traits. I have to excel to be the very best at whatever I try to do. Three other family members my only uncle, Little John; my aunt Lindsy; and her stepson, Steven normally make the arduous voyage every other year. They were also witness to the tragedy that took my dad. I am thankful at this time that I was not along because I am confident I would have attempted something stupid in an attempt to try to help him, though I know now there would have been no way to help.

This morning I arrived near the butterfish hole with a real appetite. I had not eaten very much in the past three days, something that was quite normal. I might go for a week without eating, but by then I would be really hungry. With my size, twenty-seven feet, eight inches, and a weight of seven thousand six hundred pounds, I could, shall we say, eat a horse.

My lovely Landry, who was roaming with Buffy about a mile south of my position, had found six small tuna. She and Buffy were just finishing the last one when I heard through my sonar-like telemetry what I immediately calculated to be, on and near the surface some 110 feet above me and 640 yards to my northeast, my breakfast. It was a small group of ten school tuna.

I quickly recalculated the distance and accelerated to twenty-five knots, closing the gap very quickly. This next maneuver was one of my favorites. I angled my humongous body straight up with my huge mouth wide open, now accelerating to just over thirty knots, and impacted two of the tuna, closing my mouth on both of them at the very instant my massive body broke the surface of the ocean.

    Now for the fun part. Great white sharks, like other animals, have delicate body parts. I had come completely out of the ocean some fifteen feet clear of the water. This happened just because of the velocity and the physics of my high-speed climb from over one hundred feet down. If I simply fell back into the water, I would do what humans call a belly flop and yes, it really hurts. With the kinetic energy of my seven-thousand-pound-plus body weight hitting the surface of the ocean, it could also knock the air out of my lungs. This meant I would most certainly lose the breakfast that I had just put all this effort into catching. I was not about to let that happen as I rotated my body about ninety degrees and gently reentered the ocean.

When I was only a year old, I loved to accelerate as fast as I could go, aim straight up, break the surface, and fall back in. My goal was to someday make it up to twenty feet clear of the water. My great grandfather, Nate, held the great white shark record at that time of eighteen feet. I learned to go higher and higher in my first year at jumping school. Each time, I landed harder on my stomach. My teacher, Hoyt, would get mad at me because he had to take time out from teaching the rest of the class and come over to make sure I was OK.

One day I was at least ten feet clear of the surface, and for some reason I cannot recall I twisted my body with all my strength and reentered the water on my side. I felt no discomfort or pain as I hit the surface, and I said to myself, "That was really cool, I have to try that again!" This time I went even faster, clearing the surface of the water by twelve feet. About the same time that I broke the surface, Hoyt happened to look over in my direction and yelled at the rest of the class," Ward's going to kill himself, he has to stop this jumping!" But at the top of my arc, I again twisted my body and reentered the water without any pain or discomfort.

Hoyt arrived near where I landed about the same time I did, convinced I would be in real pain and possibly unconscious. I quickly explained the maneuver that I had just invented, telling Hoyt to watch and I would do it again. I did it several more times with the same painless result. Hoyt and the entire class tried it and found that it worked for them, too. Some of my classmates who had up to this point never broken the surface were having a ball. At the end of my first school year I was awarded the school's highest achievement award. My mom and dad were very proud. I was just beginning to learn all I could.

It was now eight a.m. as the *Floodtide* backed out of her slip at the West Lake Marina in Lake Montauk. The mate, Chris, was thinking to himself that the way two of these people were drinking adult beverages, in about two hours when they started drifting in addition to chumming in the butterfish hole, they would be down below and of no help to him. They would be done for the rest of the day. He had seen this to many times before. Then again, if they got lucky and caught a good-sized fish on rod and reel, these guys would be seasick, down below and out of the way, which would be a good thing.

In the interim, the *Floodtide* made a right ninety-degree turn just outside the Lake Montauk jetties, sped up to her cruising speed of sixteen knots, and headed for the inside buoy at Shagwong Rock, now some three miles east. Eleven minutes later the *Floodtide* turned another thirty degrees right and headed for the Elbow, which lies just east of Montauk Point. From there she would head via loran C to an area just inside the butterfish hole called the CIA grounds. If you take the loran C hyperbolic lines and interpolate these numbers with latitude and longitude, the position is 40 degrees, 56 minutes, 25 seconds north; and 71 degrees, 43 minutes, 25 seconds west. This gave them an arrival time of 9:57 a.m., but as it turned out, they were destined not to make it!

✫ ✫ ✫

My Friend Michale *A true story about* THE REAL JAWS

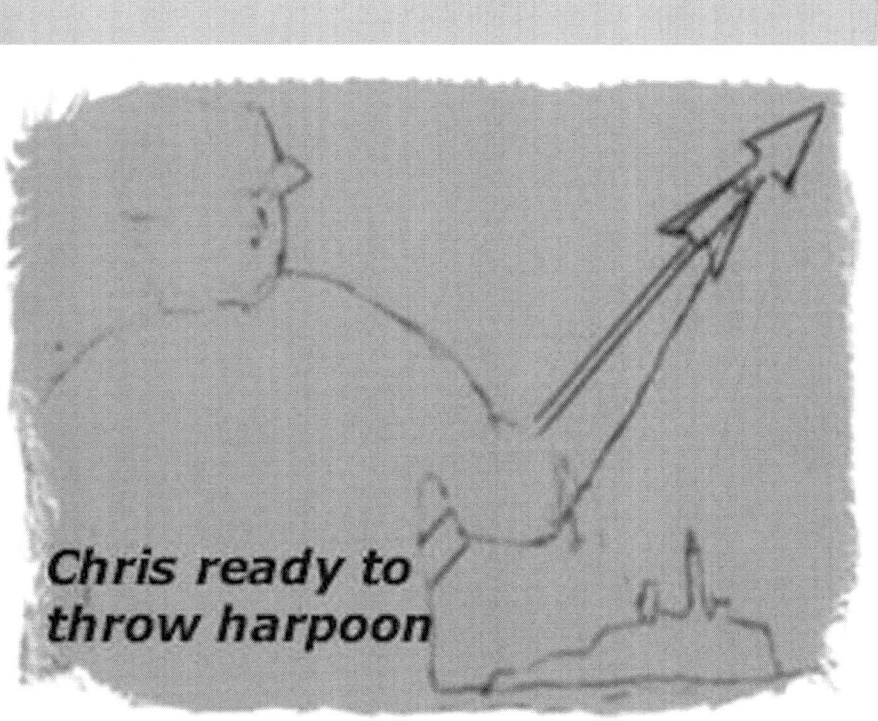

About nine thirty, for no real reason Chris went up to the bow of the *Floodtide* to look at and check the harpoon gear. This was their first trip offshore this season, and this gear had been in Sowermen's basement since last September.

The harpoon is not as sophisticated as you might think. It has a shaft or pole about ten feet long made of aluminum with a steel rod about one foot long attached at the bottom. At the top of the pole is a light piece of rope, maybe one quarter of an inch in diameter, tied through a hole in the pole. The rope is about twenty feet long so you can retrieve the handle should you have to "throw" the harpoon in order to insert the lilly into a fish.

The lilly is the business end of the gear. It is kept very sharp on the end so that it penetrates deep into tough skin and flesh. The lilly will go sideways into a fish's flesh so it will not come out the hole it made going in. There is a hole in the middle of the lilly where you can attach a one-quarter-inch stainless steel cable about two feet long with a loop on the other end. The cable is used because a rope can chafe through after a long, hard battle with a large fish, but the cable lasts with no chafing.

About halfway up the harpoon pole is a leather strap fixed to the pole. You bring the rope attached to the lilly up tight against the pole and loop the rope under the leather strap, thus keeping the lilly from falling off as you throw the harpoon at its intended target.

Attached to the cable on the *Floodtide* was three hundred feet of five- eighths polypropylene rope that would float if nothing were pulling against it. The other end was attached to a sealed thirty-gallon red barrel that floated, creating tremendous drag designed to quickly physically wear out even the largest of fish. The reason for the three hundred feet of rope is that swordfish are normally found in thirty fathoms or 180 feet of water off Montauk. With three hundred feet of rope, even a fast-moving, very large fish would not be capable of pulling the barrel under the surface. Until today.

✹ ✹ ✹

At 9:48 a.m., I computed a single school tuna near the surface 370 yards north of my position. I also computed a human boat about one hundred yards north of my breakfast.

My darling Landry saw me do my intercept calculations and realized I was about to shoot up to the surface one more time, disregarding the human boat. She immediately stopped me saying, "Don't go up, wait until the humans pass! I recall Brayden did the same thing!"

I told her not to fret: "I'm too fast, and I'll be up and back before they get here!" I redid my calculations and up I went. I came up behind the eighty-five pound tuna exactly as I had figured in my computer-like mind. My forward velocity was right at thirty-two knots as I broke the surface propelling me some eighteen feet clear of the surface with the tuna firmly in my mouth.

What I had not planned for was a boat that was about one hundred feet off my port side. I must have scared the smelly soup out of the humans, because all hell broke loose.

Chris, the man on the bow, started screaming, "MY GOD, LOOK AT THAT!" He had the presence of mind to grab on to the bow railing, knowing full well that in about five seconds a wall of green water was about to get him soaking wet as my four-ton mammoth carcass reentered the ocean.

Captain Sowermen also knew the wall of water was coming and hung on to the boat's wheel for dear life. The two people in the cockpit were not so lucky. They would both be knocked hard against the fighting chair and then down on the deck as they got soaked.

As I broke the surface, I looked over at this boat and lost my concentration on my patented reentry maneuver. I did the worst belly flop of my life, knocking myself unconscious.

Montauk point

Connecticut

Where Ward was X
harpooned

Block Island

Rhode Island

Where Michale X
freed Ward

→ **N**

Nomans land

Where Landry &
Lindsy found
Michale   X

Marthas vineyard

Chris, who was still up on the bow of the *Floodtide, was* terrified as he watched this great white shark, larger than any fish he had ever seen and by far larger than he was led to believe existed. Sowermen saw this happening and had already pulled the throttles back to idle and taken the boat out of gear. The *Floodtide* had almost stopped as it came up near this huge great white shark now lying on the surface of the water, barely moving.

Neither Chris nor Sowermen had any idea what they had just witnessed, but they were not going to waste any time until the shark revived. After making sure no one was washed overboard and all hands were OK, Sowermen started barking orders to Chris to ready the harpoon and get it into the shark as quickly as possible!

In the meantime, their charter party came up on the bridge to see what the commotion was about. Looking off the bow, they could not believe their eyes. There, just starting to move, was an unbelievably huge shark, like something out of a horror movie. It couldn't be real!

About this same time, Chris had the harpoon ready and on Sowermen's order thrust it with all his strength at the great white shark, which was now moving past the bow and starting to dive. The lilly entered just behind the four-foot-tall dorsal fin, and the polypropylene line began to go out faster and faster, as Sowermen made sure Chris stayed clear of it. He had Chris throw the barrel over the side before all the line ran out. After seeing the size of the shark he had just harpooned, Chris had the presence of mind to quickly snap on a second barrel to the first one and throw both over the side. No shark could pull two under. Now all the *Floodtide* would have to do was wait, and wait and wait.

✪ ✪ ✪

Sowermen called back to the dock in Montauk on his VHF radio to tell them he had just harpooned the largest great white shark in history and no, he was not kidding! This was, in fact, the "real" Jaws! Several other Montauk boats heard this message and right away wanted Sowermen's position and asked if he needed any help. They were on their way to his location. He replied that at this time everything was under control.

Someone back in Montauk called the local radio station, WLNG, in Sag Harbor to report this monster great white shark that had just been harpooned by a boat named the *Floodtide* south of Montauk. It was now ten fifteen a.m. By eleven, every news organization in the world was onto the story booking helicopters, chartering aircraft, and doing everything they could to get their people out to Montauk as fast as possible! By the time this evening news cycle was over, the whole world knew about this surreal event.

PART 2

Landry had heard all the commotion on the surface. When I had not returned as quickly as I had promised, she immediately sensed something was horribly wrong. Just to make matters worse, the human boat had stopped right where I reentered the water. Landry, using all her skills and knowledge, moved very carefully up towards me. Ever so slowly, I began to get my breath back and regain my senses. It could not have been more than four minutes from the time I literally crash-landed that I started swimming back down, but something very uncomfortable was now holding me back. I could feel a strange numbness and slight pain in the center of my back, again something new to me. Within two minutes of my descent I had regained all of my normal senses, as I increased my dive angle.

Just below, I could see Landry coming up to meet me. She had a strange look in her eyes. She was watching this long rope trailing along behind me.

Her immediate concern was my well-being. After swimming around me, she asked," What in heavens happened?" I started to laugh as I told her "That when I broke the surface at over thirty knots, I'd glanced over and seen the human boat much closer to me than I had calculated. I actually scared the snot out of the nose of the human on the bow of the boat and then lost my concentration while I was airborne and landed on my stomach, knocking the wind out of myself."

Landry now got very serious with me, explaining that some type of line appeared to be attached to my back, and it looked like it trailed back up to the surface. Now things began to make sense to me. The humans must have attached their device while I lay on the surface confused. It explained why I felt held back in my descent.

I asked Landry," Where is Buffy?"

Landry replied," She's still catching more of her breakfast, you know her appetite."

I thought that was great because I did not want her to see her dad in trouble with humans.

✭ ✭ ✭

Back on the surface, the people aboard the *Floodtide* were drying themselves off and assessing what had happened in the past few minutes. Captain Sowermen was informing everyone aboard that in his twenty-two years fishing Montauk waters, he had never seen a shark this size, and he had never even heard stories about anyone who claimed they had. This included anything Frank Mundus might have seen. Sowermen was positive they had the real "Jaws" on the other end of the line. *JAWS* is a movie about a huge great white shark that terrorized local beaches. It was fictional; this was not!

Chris was watching the line and the barrels, as they seemed to just be lying there; it looked to him like about one hundred feet of the rope still had not come tight. Was the shark dead? Chris was still in shock from what he had witnessed just ten minutes ago. His knees were still knocking, literally.

After Sowermen finished his briefing to the charter party, he went over to Chris, thanking him for a job very well done with the harpoon. Sowermen then discussed with the charter party why the giant shark had not taken off. No one had an answer that made any sense.

About the time they were thinking of using the boat pole to grab the line, the last one hundred feet went out faster than anyone could believe. The rope came tight, and to everyone's disbelief, both barrels disappeared below the surface like a pair of corks on a fishing rod. One second they were there, and then they were gone with no trace.

Watching the rope go out faster then he had ever witnessed, Sowermen by instinct alone jumped back on the bridge, putting the *Floodtide*'s engines into forward gear and at the same time turning the boat onto a heading in line with where the barrels had gone missing mere moments ago. When he had the boat on a course that he thought coincided with the barrels' heading, he opened the throttles on the *Floodtide* to their maximum. They were General Motors 671 diesel engines that were on governors, allowing him to run like this for hours if he needed to without harming his engines. This also gave the *Floodtide* a maximum speed of nineteen knots, which they were now doing as all hands looked for a sign of the lost barrels. This type of running was not new to Sowermen; giant tuna fishing would often require running a boat like this just to keep the fish from stripping all the line off your reel.

Sowermen then started to think to himself. This monster had just taken off for the first time and had pulled the barrels under the surface with such ease that they might never see them again. How fast was this fish capable of pulling the barrels? How long could the shark keep them below the surface? Did Sowermen have the *Floodtide* on the correct heading to follow the shark? Should he have Chris keep a lookout behind them in case the barrels surfaced behind the *Floodtide*?

In twenty-two minutes, all these questions would be answered.

✯ ✯ ✯

I had explained to Landry that I would use all of my strength, speed, and stamina to make a high-speed run and see if I could dislodge whatever the humans had attached to me.

She agreed to swim along beside me, and we were off.

I'm in the prime of my life, so on a short run, maybe five minutes, I can accelerate to thirty-five knots and sustain twenty-seven knots for thirty minutes. In addition, I can cruise at twenty knots for hours.

Landry and I accelerated to about fifteen knots as the rope attached to me came tight. I could tell right away that whatever the humans had attached to me would take all of my strength just to reach twenty-four knots. How long could

I maintain this speed? Would it be long enough to dislodge what was holding me back?

Just after reaching my top speed, Landry and I heard the human boat on the surface start running in our direction. This gave me the added incentive to do my utmost in getting some separation between us and the humans on the surface. I quickly calculated that Landry and I were going about five knots faster then the human boat. I also recognized the horrible truth that the load I was pulling was depleting my strength faster than I though possible. What had these humans done to me?

I started to comprehend the worst. I might not be able to get free of this.

What would Landry and Buffy do without me? I started to reflect on my youth, things my cousin Chase and I had learned back in history class. Great white sharks have no natural enemies. We roam the world's oceans with an under-the-sea nautical reputation as nature's perfect eating machine. The few encounters we have had with humans on boats in the past few decades have never been good. We are now taught in school to avoid humans whenever we hear or see them in boats. The few times that I have heard my ancestors speak about biting one, they always spit it out, complaining about the bad taste and the odor, which is repulsive to us. It is well known in great white shark lore that whenever we come upon them, we are to steer clear of humans and their boats. We are confident nothing good would come from an encounter with humans but of course, I had to prove my superior ability to whom, myself? Now I was entrapped in this unknown pickle. What should I do? I could always outrun, out jump, and outthink any of my classmates. But this was something I hadn't encountered before.

After fifteen minutes of pulling at the fastest speed I could maintain, just over twenty-four knots, Landry looked at me and for the first time noticed the anguish on my face. She said to me, "Nothing has changed; whatever the humans attached to you hasn't moved!"

I replied, "I'll keep going for a few more minutes; then we can stop and reassess my predicament!" I decided to stay inside the butterfish hole where the deeper water might give me an advantage over the humans. I started a right turn, as we were getting near shallow water on our present course. I also hoped the humans on the surface wouldn't know we'd turned, thus giving us even more distance away from them. This, in fact, worked; the human boat did not change course. Maybe, just maybe, they could not tell where we were.

Shortly after changing course, my strength started to weaken. Each mighty swing of my tail became less and less intense. Our speed was now down to twenty-one knots and slowing. Now I looked over at Landry, who sensed that my quickly tiring body could not keep this up much longer. I would soon have to stop and get some rest.

At the same time Landry and I both sensed two more human boats on the surface. One was headed for the human boat that had attached this thing to me. In addition, another was headed north about two miles from our present position. If the boat with the north heading did not change course soon, it would pass within one half mile of our location in about eight minutes.

I was getting desperate. I had done everything I could think of to do, and I didn't know what else to try. Suddenly,

I had an idea. I said to Landry, "Would you mind going up east towards the Vineyard and see if you could find Michale? He knows more about humans than we do; maybe he has a new idea that would help get me out of this mess! I am losing my strength too fast to keep up this speed!"

Landry said that of course she would go. She remembered Michale telling us just two days ago that we should go up east with him for the next several weeks. He had heard the feeding was nonstop for all! I quickly calculated the distance to where he should be feeding, about seventy miles from our position. If Landry could maintain her cruising speed at fifteen knots, she could be up and back in about nine-and-a-half hours. If I simply swam around slowly I should be OK for that long. We agreed to this new plan.

✡ ✡ ✡

I again asked about Buffy, and Landry said she would have to tell her, as well as Chase and Susan as she went past them. I said it would be nice to have some company as I tried to free myself from the humans. To save my strength, I slowed down to about five knots. Landry left at about twenty knots and found Chase, Buffy, and Susan. She quickly told them about my predicament and my location and our plan. Then she took up a northeasterly heading at fifteen knots and went to find Michale.

✡ ✡ ✡

My Friend Michale *A true story about* THE REAL JAWS

Mon-Tauk

*following barrels
that Ward is pulling*

Back aboard the *Floodtide*, Captain Sowermen started to wonder, *Could this monster shark simply have taken off, never to be seen again?* They were only in 180 feet of water, with three hundred feet of line on their barrels. The shark had pulled them under as if they were nothing! *Where the hell did he go? How long can he keep the barrels under? This is impossible.* He began to talk to himself. *Should I slow down? Should I speed up? I can't do that! Should I change my heading? If so, what direction? Should I just stop here and wait?*

About this same time, the charter, boat *Mon-tauk* called. "*Floodtide*, do you read me, Dave?"

✼ ✼ ✼

Captain Sowermen replied, "Yes, loud and clear, go ahead, Dan!"

"Dave, I am about three miles south of where you said you harpooned that great white shark, and about one half mile off my port side from where I'm running, two red barrels just popped up on the surface!"

Sowermen said, "That has got to be it. The barrels went under about twenty minutes ago, and we lost track of them."

Dan aboard the *Mon-tauk* replied, "OK, we will stay near them until you get here. The barrels are still going south at about five knots!"

✲ ✲ ✲

Michale and I were not only friends, we were lifelong friends. We had been born just fourteen miles south of the Moriches Inlet. Michale was born two weeks earlier than me. Michale's dad had been killed by a human fishing boat two weeks before he was born. His mother, Tracy, was killed by a Japanese long liner on the day I was born. My mom Kayla, was friends with Tracy, so the orphan Michale became my playmate the day I was born. Kayla protected baby Michale as if he were her own.

Compared to me, Michale was a runt. I was always hundreds of pounds heaver then him and several feet longer. This could have been a result of our diets. I loved almost anything. Michale, for the most part, stuck with squid, mackerel, and herring. I would call him a fickle feeder. That was fine with Michale, because it made him work harder at everything we did together. Back in school he would try to beat me in jumping class, speed class, endurance class, and most of all in thinking and judgment class. This was where Michale was the best of the best. Nobody, including our teacher, Hoyt, could hold a candle to Michale's skill when it came to solving a problem like complex intercept angles, speed needed, and distance to pray. Michale was a pure genius, always having the correct computed numbers. He simply had a gift for this. He also was one of the most tenacious fish I had ever met.

Kenneth W. Grimshaw

Floodtide at barrels

No one in or out of school would mess with Michale. He had a reputation of not backing down from anyone that tried to bully him, or as a matter of fact tried to bully me. He was just an out-and-out super friend that I could always rely on in a jam. And boy, was I in a jam!

Now, as the time started to go by much faster than I liked, my physical strength was rapidly leaving me. I started feeling sorry for myself; now more than ever I needed that friend. Just when I felt the worst, Buffy, Chase, and Susan arrived. Seeing them immediately perked me up. Within minutes, Buffy, seeing how weak I now looked, began to sob. Both Susan and Chase calmed her down, which made me feel better. I had all but stopped my forward speed.

✵ ✵ ✵

The *Floodtide* was closing in on the *Mon-tauk*'s location. Sowermen had both barrels in sight and headed directly toward the first one now only one thousand feet off the bow. It was eleven thirty as the *Floodtide* drifted alongside of the two barrels, which were moving south, but at only about one knot.

Captain Sowermen and Chris were starving, and this calm period was a perfect time to have some lunch. The men in the fishing party agreed and brought out food and drinks for all to enjoy. The *Mon-tauk* drifted along side the *Floodtide* in case Sowermen needed any help with its monster, and so lunch and banter between the two charter boats and their parties went on until one thirty, when the first of what would become many helicopters arrived over them.

Sowermen angrily waved at them to stay away, and they did back away about half of a mile and started to circle with several fixed-wing aircraft that had began to assemble. More and more boats were arriving from every direction. Within hours, this would become a full-blown Chinese fire drill. Sowermen thought, correctly, that the commotion might spook the fish.

The barrels were now moving very little and somewhat aimlessly. Sowermen told Chris that the shark might be finished. He would back the *Floodtide* down to each of the barrels, and Chris would take the boat pole and carefully bring each barrel aboard. If the rope line came in as the *Floodtide* slowly backed down, he should take in the line as long as it came easy. If the shark started to pull again, they would take several raps around the rear cleat.

"We will let the shark pull the boat instead of the barrels," Sowermen said. "That should help to kill him quickly!"

✫ ✫ ✫

Kenneth W. Grimshaw

Floodtide about to go over rope attached to Ward, center bottom of photo,barrels center right

All went well. Chris had both barrels aboard and had taken in about fifty feet of the rope when the second helicopter appears overhead with a cameraman half hanging outside, yelling "Where's the shark?"

Captain Sowermen was now furious with these clowns. He started to wave them away again when Chris yelled, "He is starting to run again! I'm taking some raps on the cleat!"

Sowermen took the *Floodtide* out of gear, but then said out loud to no one, "My god, what have we done!"

The speed of the *Floodtide* actually increased backwards.

✫ ✫ ✫

Sowermen and Chris trying to pull Ward aboard the Floodtide, as the Mon-tauk watches

MON-TAUK

Susan, Chase, Buffy and I heard the commotion up on the surface. The wop-wop was a new sound to all of us except Chase, who had heard it several times in the past, not far from their present location. Chase had seen these huge black whales, larger than anything he new that lived in the ocean pass by near the surface. Each time he witnessed one of these black monsters go by, it would have this same wop-wop, noise above. When whatever made this noise was right overhead, the harmonic resonance interfered with our sonar-like hearing.

I had barely moved for about two hours now. This had helped me regain some of my strength, and when the second helicopter arrived overhead,

I made the decision to again start moving away from the human commotion that was increasing on the surface. When I began to move my colossal tail this time, the rope came tight, and I immediately knew the humans had again done something to increase the harm they were inflicting on me. The load I was now pulling had increased fivefold.

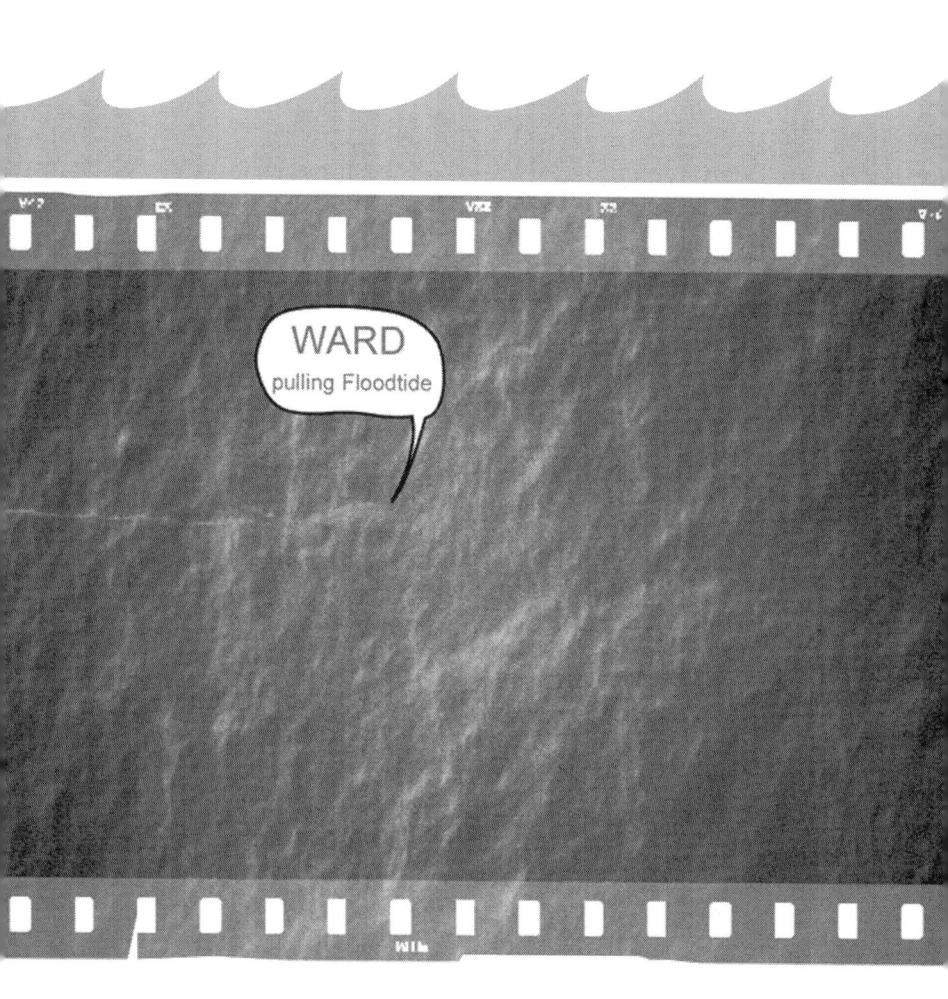

My Friend Michale *A true story about* THE REAL JAWS

PART 3

Landry had been on this heading at fifteen knots for over four hours now. She decided it was time to start searching in earnest for Michale. On her way up here, she had checked each target that fit Michael's profile, just to make sure she did not pass him by.

Just thirty minutes ago, she had come upon my aunt Lindsy. Landry quickly explained what had taken place this morning back in the butterfish hole and that she had to find Michale as fast as she could. Lindsy said she would help look for Michale, that she had seen him a few miles northeast of here only last night. They both headed that direction about three miles apart in what was fast becoming a desperate search.

On this late June afternoon, Michale was doing what he loved to do nothing! He was simply floating on the surface enjoying the sunshine. He had a full stomach from last night and was enjoying life. He'd never married, so he had few chores or duties and loved his freedom. I had explained on different occasions how my life had become so much more enjoyable since I had my own family but, Michale would shrug this off, saying maybe someday, but not now! The truth was he did not want to start a family that would put many new restrictions and responsibilities on him before he was ready.

Using her long-range sensing sonar, Landry found a possible target three miles and about twenty degrees to her starboard. Could this be Michale? It was just barely moving on the surface, Michale's favorite summertime pastime. Lindsy locked on to the same target at the same time and headed for it.

It was Michale! Landry was beside herself as she came up behind him. Michale was dozing and was startled awake as she rapidly approached him. He swung his huge body around, ready to attack whatever was closing in on his space. But he immediately recognized Landry and relaxed. She broke out in tears.

"Michale, Ward's been attacked by some humans on a boat. He asked me to see if I could find you. He thought you might have an idea that could help release him from their grasp. This all happened about six hours ago. When I left him his strength was dwindling!" It was now 4:35.

Michale said, "The time is too critical to waste. I will go back with you girls. Landry, set up a course using a speed of fifteen knots, and we can maintain that for the next four or more hours!"

Landry said, "Yes, that's the speed I used on my way up here looking for you!"

Lindsy agreed; she was coming also and could help comfort Buffy, who was much too young to be witnessing the brutal torture her father was going through.

Lindsy started to tear up as they got underway. She had been present when Brayden went through this same thing when the human boat *Crickett II* killed him. What I must be going through had to be at the very least unnerving for little Buffy.

✯ ✯ ✯

The *Mon-tauk* was fast becoming the center where all the media congregated. There was now a full-blown armada of boats on the scene. Captain Sowermen had spoken to the Montauk Coast Guard earlier, telling them that there were so many helicopters and airplanes around, he hoped they would not run into each other. *Point Wells*, the Montauk Coast Guard's eighty-five footer, had also arrived to try to keep some form of order and a safe distance between the boats. The media was looking for any information that the *Floodtide* could give them. The radio chatter became impossible to understand just nonstop diatribe.

It was now three thirty. Captain Sowermen had attached the harpoon line directly to the stern of the *Floodtide* about two hours ago. The monster shark had towed the *Floodtide* about four miles northeast from where it had been harpooned, and the boat was still moving northeast at about two knots. The shark had not changed course or speed since they had tied the rope to the boat; it seemed almost eerie as Sowermen began to think to himself that the shark was on a mission.

Two of Sowermen's fishing party were still consuming adult beverages. The ocean had been calm most of the day, but now the ten-to fifteen-mile-an-hour southwest land breeze made it choppy. The *Floodtide* was being towed stern first to the northeast. This put the chop on their port side. Both of the men started to heave at the same time. Chris said to himself, "What took so long! "The men then went down below, and Chris was left to swab up the mess. The other two members were, for the most part, well behaved and stayed up on the bridge with Captain Sowermen.

✵ ✵ ✵

My condition continued to deteriorate. It was now five o'clock as I struggled on this heading. With each swing of my mighty tail, I became weaker. Could I keep up even this slow pace until Landry returned? Had she found Michale? After four hours, would she simply turn around and return without him? Was she even on her way back, or was she still looking for him? What would it be like to die?

These thoughts were tearing me apart inside. None of this would be taking place if I had listened to Landry's common sense request.

The human boat noise from above was taking a toll of its own on my great white shark family as we milled around below. On a normal day when we heard boat propeller noise, we would move away from it.

The ever-present harmonic beating from the boats propeller blades interfered with our sonar like hearing. It was simple to just stay clear of the human boats. Now there was a large group of them assembled overhead, which made it very difficult to do normal distance calculations. The constant wop-wop-wop from the helicopters made my mind as tired as my body. How much more of this could I take?

Despite being the leader of my family, someone they all looked up to, I began to sob to myself. By taking a foolish gamble, I'd put my life in danger. Should I live through this horror, I promised myself that I would think through any task before taking it on! I would never again let any member of my family near a human boat! I'd never dreamed that I could be so humbled like this, let alone in front of my precious daughter.

Thank god for these thoughts; they gave me a newfound will to live. My tail began moving in a stronger motion then it had in the past hour. The humans would not beat me. I had a whole new will to survive. It was 7:25 p.m. as I regained my newfound will to beat the humans that were trying to kill me.

DESPERATION had been turned into DETERMINATION. I calculated that as I had weakened the past few hours and had not pulled very hard, the humans had shortened the line between their boat and me to about one hundred and fifty feet. I would not let them get any closer. I would swim as hard as I could so they could not retrieve any more rope! If they succeeded in killing me, it would be from this distance! Where was Landry? She would be proud of my newfound will to survive!

Landry, Michale, and Lindsy could hear and sense the tumult about five miles ahead of them. They could also sense the targets below the tumult; this had to be the rest of the family with me. They were about twelve miles closer than when Landry had left me. Knowing me, she was convinced I had spent all this time coming in her direction to help shorten her voyage. The three of them increased their speed to flank. It would still take them until 8:10 to arrive at my location.

✫ ✫ ✫

All day, Sowermen had a good feeling about ultimately catching this larger-than-life great white shark. From early this morning when they first harpooned it until now, everything had been going the *Floodtide*'s way. But in the past twenty minutes, he had begun to wonder.

He asked Chris, "Is it me, or has our backwards speed increased in the past fifteen or twenty minutes?"

Chris replied, "I have been thinking the same thing. The waves have increased against the transom, but the wind seems to be lighter!"

Sowermen added "After all this, instead of getting weaker, he has gotten stronger!"

✫ ✫ ✫

All of the national news programs would lead their broadcasts the same way: "Monster great white shark harpooned off Montauk, Long Island, New York! The battle of the boat that harpooned this real 'Jaws' seventeen miles south of Montauk at ten this morning continues!" They then switched to helicopters with live reporters giving their opinions of what was or wasn't happing. They had reporters live in Montauk at various boat docks giving nonstop interviews that ran from guessing about the size of the great white shark to how aggressive they were to plain out-and-out nonsense. The question they asked everyone was, "Is this all just a hoax?"

A lot of the quote "Experts" had never seen a great white shark, let alone caught one or been near one for that matter. All these new "experts" were divided as to the size this great white shark might be. But there they were, in living color giving interviews to the entire world about something they knew nothing about. This type of reporting had made great white sharks into monsters that should be removed from the oceans around the world. It was shameful.

✡ ✡ ✡

Aboard the *Floodtide*, Captain Sowermen no longer shared these views. In the past ten or so hours, he had formed the exact opposite opinion. He had developed nothing but admiration and respect for one of Mother Nature's greatest creations. The great white shark was without question the ocean's most amazing, strongest, and he was beginning to believe, possibly smartest fish in the ocean. Everything they had tried as a crew to bring this great white shark to the boat had failed.

✭ ✭ ✭

It was eight fifteen, and just in front of me I sensed for the first time three targets coming toward me at a very fast rate. "Please be Landry!" I cried out. It was Landry, with Lindsy by her side, and Michale right behind. I was overjoyed. I'd survived. I did not know how, but I had until she returned with help!

My Friend Michale *A true story about* THE REAL JAWS

MICHALE

Michale quickly said hello to everyone, looked at me, and immediately realized how critical my situation was. Time was of the essence! If I were to survive this ordeal, he would have to find a solution now.

Michale backed off slowly at first, and then began to circle me. He gave no one a clue as to what he was up to or why. His speed increased as his circle got bigger. He was now about one hundred yards from me when he turned towards my tail. He was doing at least twenty knots when he moved his huge bill and with unbelievable strength cut the five-eighths rope like it was a piece of string. Using his forward velocity and moving his head, made his triangular shaped, razor sharp bill a lethal weapon of untested strength. No wonder Swordfish had no natural enemies.

I was free! My friend Michale, a swordfish, had saved his best friend's life.

✭ ✭ ✭

On board the *Floodtide*, the transom rose a foot as the rope went slack and slowly floated to the surface. Chris pulled in the lose line as it floated on the surface of the ocean. When he reached the end of the floating rope he gasped out loud, "Captain look at this"! Sowermen came over to look at the end of the rope Chris was holding. There was no Lilly, it had not pulled free. There was no evidence of the rope chafing against something. It had not simply broken, or parted, it clearly had been CUT!

Sowermen knew immediately that the shark had been freed and was gone but how? He said out loud, so every one aboard could hear him, "The shark won, fair and square. I for the love of me don't know how, but the shark won!"

That evening on his way back to the dock in Montauk, Captain Sowermen became a different man. He was contrite as he realized what had taken place. From around 1:30 that afternoon until about 8:25, his boat had been towed backwards on an east-northeast course, about 14 miles, against a westerly set of over one knot.

He vowed to himself that he would never again have a harpoon on his boat. He could not bear the thought of letting himself be tempted to try and kill one of these amazing animals again.

✫ ✫ ✫

Kenneth W. Grimshaw

Michale as he cuts Wards harpoon line, freeing him from the Floodtide

The following winter, at every Montauk Boatman's Association meeting Sowermen would lobby all his fellow charter boat captains to join him, and do the same. None of them ever would. Their charter boat season was too short and the simple economics of their business demanded they have any and all possible avenues of revenue open to them. This included finding the occasional swordfish and harpooning it for the cash.

✡ ✡ ✡

The news media didn't quit. Dozens stayed in Montauk for the next few weeks, chartering boats and airplanes, all hoping for a glimpse of this monster shark.
The interviews were never ending, as the stories grew. There were some excellent photos taken showing a huge great white shark with and obvious mark just behind the dorsal fin.

✫ ✫ ✫

I recovered in less than two weeks with no ill effects. I still have something tickling my back when I turn sharply. Michale stayed near my family and me during my convalescence. There are many makos in these waters, and in my weakened state, as mean and nasty as this shark can be, a group of them might try to attack me. With Michale nearby they would never try.

Kenneth W. Grimshaw

WARD 8 days later

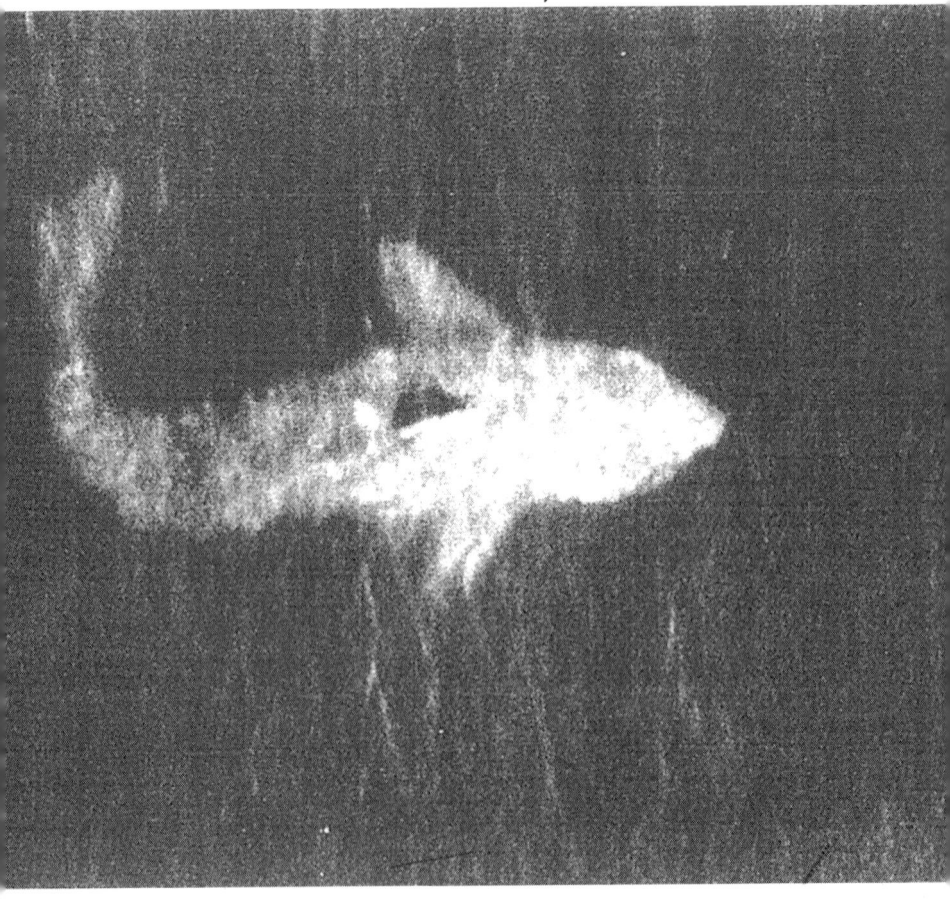

✿ ✿ ✿

However, within a year my family would suffer a fatal tragedy at the hands of the humans! The human news media would be, if possible, even more involved! Stay tuned for more of my adventures!

AUTHOR BIOGRAPHY

The author, a native East Hampton Bonacker, is a fifteen thousand hour airline transport rated pilot. He had the utmost privilege for years, of meeting and flying America's Who's Who! He than spent the other half of his life flying a Super Cub off Montauk, L.I., N.Y., spotting Swordfish, Giant Tuna, Whales, and Great White Sharks! During this time frame he was also the captain of sport fishing boats catching many of these same game fish! In the summer of 1978, he was the only one to capture visible photographs of a Great White Shark that had been harpooned that same day. In Mr. Grimshaw's photos taken from his fish spotting Super Cub, the shark is visible under water! His photos were used by none other than Walter Cronkite on the CBS evening news that night! He was also interviewed on NBC's Today Show by Jane Pauley! One of his Great White Shark photos was on the front page of the New York Daily News! Nick Karas, Newsday's chief sports writer interviewed, fished with, and wrote about Mr. Grimshaw several times that summer. Peter Benchley (The author of "JAWS") fished with Mr. Grimshaw for over a week! He then received his fifteen minutes of fame with Curt Gowdy which led to a one hour ABC American Sportsman episode! These Great White Shark capers led to his appearances on other American Sportsman shows, also morning TV shows, and many newspaper interviews and articles!